Finely Ground Goodness

Comfort and Healing Devotionals

Belinda John, D.D.

Copyright © 2013 -- Dr. Belinda John

All rights reserved. No part of this document may be reproduced or transmitted in any form or by any means, electronic, mechanical, photocopying, recording, or otherwise, without prior written permission of Divine Works Publishing.

Biblical scripture quotations are taken from King James Version, unless otherwise stated. All emphasis within Scripture quotations is the author's own.

Divine Works Publishing
Wellington, Florida 33414
(561)247-1359

To book author for speaking engagements call (561)247-5402.

Acknowledgements

I'd like to first thank God the Father, Christ the Son, and the Holy Spirit for being the sole reason for my existence and for being the first real love of my life. For being that divine expression of unconditional love that had the power to heal me in all my broken parts, and in whom I now live and move and have my being.

I'd like to also thank my husband, Dr. Sheldon F. John, a Godly man whom God entrusted my life's purpose with. A man who met me while I was in a dead place in life, and who breathed life into mine. A man who took one look at me and my children and decided to be the void that was missing in our lives. God heard my prayers and answered them in the form of you.

My children Tyra, Every, and Keenen, who are the lights of my life. You bring me continual joy and purpose. I am extremely proud of you all. I read once that when God gives you children is like he takes out a piece of your heart and allows it live, breathe, and walk outside of you. You are all just that—my heart. I could not imagine life without you!

My parents, Frank and Candida Figueroa, and my sisters Angela and Brenda. You all helped to shape who I am today, I could not have asked for a better family to be born into. You taught me the meanings behind God, love and family. Thank you, can only begin to express my gratitude and appreciation.

My Shulamite Women Family, a group of powerfully dynamic women who make me strive to be the very best I can be, I am so grateful for you all.

My spiritual covering Drs. Renny and Marina Mclean, there aren't enough thank you's to express what you mean to us and all that has come forth via our connection to you. Thank you for allowing us to see God through your eyes when we couldn't fully see Him through our own.

Dedication

This book is dedicated to my Grandmother,
Felicita Arroyo Guitard.
Your warm smile and unyielding selflessness
will always be remembered.

Contents

Introduction..*10*
Out of the Old, Into the New.....................................*13*
In Him Will I Trust..*17*
Raising A Standard..*21*
An Acceptable Attitude..*25*
A Contrite Heart..*29*
Whose Battle is it Anyway?.......................................*33*
A Friend is He..*33*
Transformational Power..*41*
Knowing the Truth..*45*
Out of Darkness, Into the Light................................*49*
Releasing Offense...*53*
Jealous Roots..*57*
Letting Go..*61*
Are you Filled?...*65*
Which Right is Wrong?...*69*
"Christ-Like" Love..*73*
A Little Leaven..*77*
The Father's Will...*81*
Fear Not!..*85*
Figuring the Pay Off..*89*
Release the Anointing..*93*
Notes..*98*

Introduction

For what seemed like a very long and painful period of time, life itself just didn't seem to make much sense at all to me. Somehow, what I knew —not an intellectual conscience knowing, but a still quiet knowing that existed deep inside of me—didn't quite line up with what I was experiencing around me. For years, one failed attempt and disappointment after another surfaced until I was left completely depleted: emotionally, spiritually, relationally and financially. Somehow, I knew that I was due better, but I didn't quite know how to materialize those things in my life.

What I finally learned behind all those lessons was to listen and honor that still small voice which had been speaking within me. I learned that life had a mysterious way of honoring me back when I had the courage to prioritize *that voice* above all others. I say courage because I have learned that most people won't understand, agree, or like you when you decide to honor the authentic you. The real you that was created before you were formed in the womb of your mother, the one that refuses to hide behind facades, masks, and ego.

I learned that because some people are still entrapped in their own vicious inner pain cycles, that they are unable to fully embrace the ones who have found freedom living from their place of authenticity. I believe it is a painful reminder of what they are lacking, and some, rather than try to attain it for themselves, would rather avoid, attack, or criticize.

I also learned that although the people closest to us may have good intentions for us, what we need individually to become who we really are is not learned from anyone other than the Holy Spirit. Things took a turn for the better when I inclined my ear to the understanding of His voice. It wasn't that I no longer listened to people, but that I learned to hear when the Spirit of God was present in what was being spoken and when it wasn't.

Today, I share this believer's devotional journal with you in hopes that the spiritual truths that have helped augment my understanding and enhance my life, would equally enrich yours, and encourage you to grow in a deeper relationship with Jesus Christ.

I encourage you to visit each devotional twice daily, in order to help frame your day with the word of God. In the morning time, read a devotional and spend a few moments in reflective prayer and meditation; in the evening time revisit the same devotional from that morning. Review the days events and recall the opportunities that presented themselves to apply each principle, and then proceed to journal about them. You will begin to notice that when you focus your intention on expressing one of the principles mentioned that life will bring forth an opportunity for you to implement it. Life is the platform whereby all our deepest dramas, fears, and beliefs play themselves out.

Follow the instructions *"write about what you thought would happen, what actually happened, what you learned, and what you would do differently the next time"*.

I begin with *what you thought would happen* because many people allow an imagined fear that tells them that things won't work out or they will mess up or look foolish to stop them from trying. I've learned to say so what? I'd rather try and risk looking foolish (which really never turned out to be the case) than to be crippled by fear. This first step is so critical because it allows you to see for yourself and have your own experiences. Most times what you thought would happen and what really happen are two totally different scenarios. Journaling these events will help to reinforce your belief in yourself and help you to overcome some of your fear based behaviors.

If at any time the principle is especially challenging for you, and some should be, just repeat it again the next day and as long as you need to after that. The purpose of this devotionals journal is that you actually get something out of it, not that you race to complete it.

Just like buying an exercise bike won't do anything for you unless you actually mount it and use it, the exercises within this devotional journal are also meant to be applied, and used in your life. If you really want to experience transformational results just reading this book isn't going to be enough. You will need to apply and reapply what you learn.

Out of the Old, Into the New

"Therefore, if any man be in Christ, he is a new creature: old things are passed away; Behold, all things are become new."
2 Corinthians 5:17

Up until the time we experience our rebirth in Christ we have only seen and experienced life through our earthly nature, but once we hand over our lives to Christ we are continuously being taught and trained by the Holy Spirit to experience life in a new way. We are transformed from something old and limited, into a new creature with supernatural ability (provided to us by the power of the Holy Spirit). The breathe of the Almighty is breathed upon us and new realms of understanding, once closed off, are made accessible to us.

But it is the spirit in a person, the breath of the Almighty, that gives them understanding. Job 32:8 [1] (NIV)

Our spiritual mind becomes awakened and we become perceptively aware of the infinite amount of choices and resources available to us that we were once clueless to. So, on the exterior we look exactly the same, but something in our inward most parts —in our spirit— is radically changed, and although initially the change may not be obvious, life will soon become the stage where this newness unfolds.

Becoming a new creature is such a powerful concept. It means that although I was born a certain way, to a certain family, and into a certain set of circumstances, my newness in Christ affords me the opportunity to be radically transformed out of the usual or expected outcome. Think about that for a moment, there are no limitations to who we can become. Nothing that already exists can properly define the potential we have living on the inside of us. It's unique to each one of us and afforded to us by divine design.

Although this is a great revelation, we still have a major part to play in how this is expressed within our lives and to the extent that we will allow the new creation that we are in Christ to live and flow through us.

Spiritual discipline is key here. Since it is "in" our spirit that we are changed, then it is our spirit man that needs to be nourished and fortified, and what we fill it with today determines what our lives will reflect tomorrow. Much like our physical bodies, when we eat the wrong stuff, it shows! If we are going to be truly transformed into that new creature, that is in the likeness of Christ, we must fill ourselves with the word of God, for Christ was the word made flesh. He didn't come just to teach it, but to demonstrate it. In that same manner, we must not be hearers only but doers of the word. It's not enough to know and recite this stuff, it must be applied and worked into our lives continually.

Applying the word to our situations takes Faith, it means we trust God at the level of His word, that simply because He stated it, then we can bank on it. That's relational! Its takes confidence in God's ability and in His promises to see you through to the end, but he *will* meet your faith. He is faithful. Meaning you bring your faith, (your hopes, dreams, and desires coupled with your belief in Him) and he fulfills it. That's exciting, no matter what level of faith you are at!

Therefore I tell you, whatever you ask for in prayer, believe that you have received it, and it will be yours. (Mark 11:24)

I recall struggling, during my initial years in the Lord, with understanding exactly what faith was. I knew that I desperately wanted to see change in my life, but it was a concept I really couldn't get a grasp of. It was foreign to my old way of being and thinking. Then the Lord challenged me and put before me a decision to accomplish something I never imagined I'd be able to. It was something I thought was out of my reach, but God whispered into my heart that if I would have faith in His ability and not my own, that he would bring it to fruition. I believed him and he was true to His word.

Prayer and Meditation Scripture: I can do all things through Christ, which strengtheneth me (Philippians 4:13).

Morning Assignment: As you meditate on the scripture above, embrace the understanding that everything we are designed to be, all the potential we have stored on the inside of us, is operating at peak when we exchange our old thoughts, patterns, and beliefs for His absolute truths. Jesus said "I am the way, the truth, and the life. By examining the thoughts that consume most of your thinking and guide your behavior, and replacing them with higher ways of thinking you will experience a new, beautiful, and divinely inspired, one-of- a-kind you!

To help examine and identify some of your faulty thought patterns review and answer the following questions, be as honest as you can when answering them to help you asses which areas to focus on.

- How much time do spend worrying about bad things happening to you or those you love?
- Are you overly critical of yourself and others?
- Do you call others to recount and re-live the bad things that have happened to you?
- Do you wish bad things on those that you are angry with?
- Do you compare yourself to others ?
- Do you allow yourself to be angry for prolonged periods of time?
- How do you handle change?
- How do you handle conflict?
- How do you feel around people who are more successful, smarter, attractive than you believe yourself to be? And why do you feel that way?
- What are your relationships like? Are they for the most part happy and healthy? Or are they mostly stressful?

Reflecting on your answers above, and your own individual experiences, would you say that most of your day is framed around more positive or negative thoughts? If you answered negative, you are not alone, most people think this way until the truth washes away the residue of the old creature and all the lies it once believed. Now that you have identified some weak areas, take action! **Begin by replacing each negative behavior with a more desirable one.** Imagine yourself becoming that person. Remember you can be that person because your trust is in Christ and not in yourself. God's word reminds us that *His strength is made perfect in our weakness. (2 Corinthians 12:9)*

If you have made it this far, take a moment to congratulate yourself. No, really do it! It takes true determination to value yourself, be honest with yourself, and work on improving yourself, but know this, YOU are so worth every minute spent on you!

---

1. New International Version

Evening Journal:

*Reflect on Your Morning Assignment and note what happened today as a result of you trying something new. Write about what you **thought** would happen, what **actually** happened, what you **learned**, and what you would do **differently** the next time.*

In Him Will I Trust

For I will not trust in my bow, neither shall my sword save me. Psalm 44:6

We have a responsibility to do our part and the Lord faithfully does His. King David, being a skilled swordsman knew better than to rely on his own sword to save him, and although his reputation for being a mighty warrior preceded him, he didn't allow that to go to his head. Instead, he humbly acknowledged the source of his strength. He knew the difference between what he was able to do alone and what he was able to do with God by his side. There were also times, prior to engaging battle, that he would inquire of the Lord if this was something he should pursue. He understood far too well what being outside of the will of God could lead to.

Socially, we've been taught to become self-reliant and to bypass seeking God for guidance and direction. We move at a rapid pace, we inundate our own schedules, and often times take on more than we can handle. However, we must be cautious how we approach opportunities and open doors in our lives. Not every open door is one meant for us to walk through, and without proper spiritual discernment we can suffer more things than we ought to.

Self motivations and skewed perspectives can easily cause us to not see the potential dangers that lie ahead. There will be times when the deception is so subtle, we won't even realize we are being led astray. The danger lies in that we can begin to put our trust, expectations, and hope in the wrong things.

Remember the enemy employs indistinct tactics, and therfore is very good at convincing us to tune out the voice of the Holy Spirit. Other times, we tune out His voice, simply because what the Spirit is telling us we would rather not hear. Once we discharge the Holy Spirit from our decision making, it is at this time that demonic seeds are planted and we are no longer under the protection of God. We won't always want to admit it but this is where misfortunes hit our lives. We must be willing to take personal responsibility for our thought life and renew our minds daily with His word and seek Him first, if we desire to win life's battles.

> ***Prayer and Meditation Scripture:*** I will say of the LORD, He is my refuge and my fortress: my God; in him will I trust. (Psalms 91:2)

Morning Assignment: As you pray and meditate on the above scripture *ask God to reveal the areas where he may want you to trust Him in; where He might want to stretch you.* Usually the answer involves doing something new, something different, out of the norm, and/or out of your comfort zone. Listen for the answer, maybe a memory will pop in your mind, or a desire you once had will rekindle, or an new idea will surface. It's usually a very soft and gentle type of reminder, a still small voice from within, and it may sometimes not appear until later in the day or week. Just know that once you have set your intention, God will reply.

Once you have identified where the Lord is leading you, take note of the areas that might seem challenging, and wherever there is a struggle, pay special attention to. Usually the areas with great resistance also yield the greatest breakthroughs. As you journal in the evening ask the Lord to reveal what the struggles are about. You will be able to pin-point with greater clarity the areas in which the Lord wants you to trust him in and why you are having issues letting go in that area. You can start off by asking yourself "What are you scared of?"

It's important during this time to be patient with yourself, you are just getting clear here, it's about being honest with yourself, it's *not* about forcing yourself to do anything you're not comfortable doing, it's about uncovering the real hidden fears that are keeping you from moving forward and learning how to lean into God more in these areas. If it becomes too difficult put it down for now, and return to the exercise again. Give yourself permission to do this as many times as it takes. It is normal for this to take some time so just keep an open heart and mind until you gain the understanding. Take a deep breath and simply put your trust in Him. He's got you!

Evening Journal:

*Reflect on Your Morning Assignment and note what happened today as a result of you trying something new. Write about what you **thought** would happen, what **actually** happened, what you **learned**, and what you would do **differently** the next time.*

Raising A Standard

"When the enemy shall come in like a flood, the Spirit of the LORD shall lift up a standard against him." (Isaiah 59:19)

Deciding to serve God, certainly comes with its fair share of challenges. Life, at times, can feel weighty and overwhelming. During these times we need not only know scripture, but we must be cognizant of the lesson at hand. The enemy will surely come disguised, ready to deceive, and with an ultimate agenda to destroy. However, once the Lord reveals a battle strategy, we will learn how to obtain sweet victory in each of life's difficulties. Because the Lord's ways are not our own —his ways are higher — it's imperative that we seek guidance from Him in the greater and in the lesser things. He desires to enlighten us to war by the spirit, and not by the flesh, so embracing his standards becomes essential for our survival.

The rhema understanding of this particular scripture was imparted into my life sort of indirectly. It was at the time that a dear girlfriend of mine experienced an attack against her marriage in the form of infidelity. Like many other couples, who throughout different times may have some unsettled resentments or regrets, it seemed the perfect excuse to her husband to continue being lured by this other woman. After all, we should all be happy, right? Wrong! What we all should be is obedient to the Father's will whether it's comfortable or not, because what we desire for ourselves is not always God's best for us.

So, during my prayer time I began to seek the Lord for answers on her behalf. He gave me the scripture above, but I was uncertain of how it applied. As I continued to press in, the Lord revealed to me that for years, my girlfriend had been a good Godly wife; she had attended to all her husband's needs, cooked his meals, washed his clothes, and packed his lunch daily, amongst many of the other ways in which she demonstrated her love for him. The Lord then began to show me how not all women serve their husbands in this capacity and that the woman whom he was having the affair with was not a subservient type of woman. The Lord proceeded to share that because my girlfriend had raised a standard, that this other woman could not fit the bill. Because of the standard she had set for her marriage, her husband would not leave her, despite the many relentless attempts of the other woman to divide them. As we continued to press in prayer, her husband began to see the deception for himself, and in the areas he once believed that he had outgrown the marriage, he began to doubt himself, and his decisions. He began disclosing his heart to his wife, and chose to put an end to the affair. His wife chose to forgive him. The other woman did not take this well and became quite a nuisance to them both for the months that ensued. Her negative behavior and deceitful tactics further reinforced his decision for his wife and strengthened their union. I am happy to know that years later their marriage is still strong and that they both grew tremendously during this battle.

On a personal level this experience taught me that the greatest warfare against the enemy is demonstrated through how we conduct ourselves in the small things we do daily. Who would have ever known that a lifestyle of attending to her husbands needs would wage war against the enemy and would become a shield of protection in the thick of the battle?

Prayer and Meditation Scripture: For we wrestle not against flesh and blood, but against principalities, against powers, against the rulers of the darkness of this world, against spiritual wickedness in high places. (Ephesians 6:12)

Morning Assignment: Learning how to war in the spirit is for the mature minded. It requires a dedication to understanding the will of God and an obedience in our daily walk. As you move forth today become aware of your routine. Where could you reach a little further outside of yourself for those around you? Perhaps for family members, children, neighbors, or coworkers? Close your eyes for a few minutes and as you meditate begin to see yourself taking a few extra moments each day to express kindness, generosity, lending a hand, or simply saying a prayer for someone else. Set your intention to raise the standard in all the different circles you engage in. Remember it's our small daily decisions that begin to shape our future and do the greatest damage against the works of Satan.

Evening Journal:

*Reflect on Your Morning Assignment and note what happened today as a result of you trying something new. Write about what you **thought** would happen, what **actually** happened, what you **learned**, and what you would do **differently** the next time.*

An Acceptable Attitude

For what glory is it, if, when ye be buffeted for your faults, ye shall take it patiently? but if, when ye do well, and suffer for it, ye take it patiently, this is acceptable with God. 1 Peter 2:20

I can recall of times when I was completely baffled by the harsh treatment of others when attempting to do something that I felt was right. Early during my Christian walk this was one of the most difficult lessons for me to grasp, yet one of the most powerful ones.

The truth is that many ugly, ungodly, and down-right nasty personalities will surface along your life's journey. You must know that this is part of the process and that even in the midst of those unpleasant situations, God still requires something from you.

During these times, I was being taught what was pleasing and acceptable to God. It was with His abundant grace that I began to grow in my understanding. I began to notice how situations and individuals which usually would send me into an emotional orbit, would no longer move me, and that with the understanding of His truths, I could always *choose* to abide in His peace. I learned how to regain my personal power and to use it in a way that was constructive. Being under the grace of God didn't mean that I would not have to go into the lion's den, or weather some serious storms, but It did mean that he gave me His peace and serenity through it all, and more importantly that I no longer had to be the type of person that would be moved by these situations. I could simply *choose* a different response. I discovered that the real issue isn't the adversity that comes our way, but how we *choose* to handle it.

Prior to being enlightened to this new understanding, I had always been the type of person who would easily admit my wrongs and deal with the consequences if I had made a mistake—but if I was innocent—now, that was a different story... I would be ready to fight until the bitter end. I believe many of you can relate to this but, now in Christ, I am no longer consumed with being right. I am more concerned with being used by God, even if just to change the perspective of one person towards God. We can do a lot more damage to the kingdom of darkness by being more peaceable than right.

Well-doing in the Lord doesn't always appear as we would prefer, in fact, it comes with quite a bit of self-sacrifice. However, in this place of suffering, God teaches us to see past the initial discomfort and into the deeper areas that need to be healed within—both in us and in others. Sometimes it's going to take walking away from an argument, or turning the other cheek, or even just surrendering control of the situation. Putting it, (whatever "it" maybe) into God's hands, because He can do so much more than we ever could.

Remember that people long for authentic love, despite how much they may project something entirely different. Genuine, soul-to-soul, connection is necessary for healthy human development. When you incorporate this understanding into your daily walk, the impact you make grows exponentially. It's in the difficult places, that God desires to shine *His* light and in which he desires to use you greatly. Although not always the easiest thing to do, expressing Godly character as opposed to our own, certainly is the more rewarding thing to do.

Prayer and Meditation Scripture: Wherefore let them that suffer according to the will of God commit the keeping of their souls to him in well doing, as unto a faithful Creator. (1 Peter 4:19)

Morning Assignment: Notice how God calls suffering according to the will of God, well-doing. As you move forth today set your intention to change someone's view of God, it may cost you being right, being acknowledged, or at times even being liked. However, the reward of well-doing according to the will of God, will take you to depths in God that your natural mind could never comprehend. Close your eyes for a few minutes and as you meditate on the above scripture begin to feel yourself radiating peace, enduring suffering for the sake of expressing that peace, and stepping into dark uncomfortable situations to be a reflection of His light, love, and hope. As you envision yourself becoming one with this peace, opportunities to express His heart will begin to open up before you throughout the day. Seize each moment and sacrifice that you might endure a little suffering for doing that which God deems good.

Evening Journal:

*Reflect on Your Morning Assignment and note what happened today as a result of you trying something new. Write about what you **thought** would happen, what **actually** happened, what you **learned**, and what you would do **differently** the next time.*

A Contrite Heart

And David's heart smote him after that he had numbered the people. And David said unto the Lord, I have sinned greatly in that I have done: and now, I beseech thee, O Lord, take away the iniquity of thy servant; for I have done very foolishly. 2 Samuel 24:10

Today's scripture reveals one of the main reasons, I believe, God loved King David so. It discloses David's reverent heart before the Lord, and his willingness to be wrong and humbled.

Here within the text, we learn that for whatever reason King David, in preparation for battle, despite the fervid protests of Joab and all the captains of his militia, decides to number his army. So rather than consult with Jehovah, who had faithfully brought him through so many past victories, he decides instead to rely on military strength to bring him through. The bible does not detail his reasoning, but we can gather from the text, that this move was a foolish move in that it:

1. Angered the Lord
2. Was opposed by his entire army leadership
3. Cost him a hefty price

Perhaps, it was pride that the Lord was exposing in him. More strikingly however, is his displayed abasement, acknowledgement of sin, responsibility by not blaming others, and willingness to take personal ownership of the outcome by making restitution as quickly as possible. I am all too familiar with those places in our lives when we decide to make self-guided decisions. Not all *good* decisions are *God's* plan or intention for us, and we can find ourselves being led down similar paths. If we are going to truly allow the greatness of God's glory to manifest in our lives, then we must acknowledge Him in ALL our ways, allow him to direct our paths and decisions.

His ways are not our ways, and we therefore cannot always understand what he is doing in and through our lives. Yet still, it is this human desire to rationalize what he is doing, which becomes one of the major hindrances to walking out our individual God-given destinies. The more this human reasoning takes place, the longer it takes for God's will to flourish in our lives. Sometimes God does not require us to understand His will, but to Trust him— even when it seems unreasonable.

Its not a guessing game, the bible tells us that His spirit bears witness with our spirit. It is the Holy Spirit of God that reveals the mind of God to us (1 Corinthians 2:10-13). A contrite heart doesn't mind waiting on an answer from the Lord, for it knows that to do otherwise is foolish.

> ***Prayer and Meditation Scripture:*** The Lord is nigh unto them that are of a broken heart; and saveth such as be of a contrite spirit (Psalms 34:18).

Morning Assignment: For today, make a choice to acknowledge the Lord in all your decisions, even in the small ones. Begin to inquire of him, in areas which you normally wouldn't. He may have something very special waiting for you. As you move forth today, set your intention to be willing to do things God's way, which means it may not be your usual comfortable route. Once you set your intention, the opportunity will present itself throughout the day, be careful not to miss it when it does! Learn to slow down and begin to rely on Him, He will show you things that you would otherwise miss. Slowing down not only means your daily activities, but to slow down your inner most being, and to quiet all the internal noises, so that you can decipher His voice and follow His instructions. As you pray and meditate on the above scripture, request that the Lord give you a special ear today to hear Him, that your heart be contrite and lowly before him, so that you can learn to allow Him to govern your decisions. As a result of allowing Him to guide you daily, you will begin to see your life take a completely different form and direction. When you fail to do so or feel you've fallen off, simply ask for forgiveness and like David confess before the Lord: *O Lord take away the iniquity of thy servant; for I have done very foolishly.* Know that he forgives you the moment you ask Him.

Evening Journal:

*Reflect on Your Morning Assignment and note what happened today as a result of you trying something new. Write about what you **thought** would happen, what **actually** happened, what you **learned**, and what you would do **differently** the next time.*

Whose Battle is it Anyway?

And the sun stood still, and the moon stayed, until the people had avenged themselves upon their enemies. Is not this written in the book of Jasher? So the sun stood still in the midst of heaven, and hasted not to go down about a whole day. And there was no day like that before it or after it, that the LORD hearkened unto the voice of a man: for the LORD fought for Israel. Joshua 10:13-14

What exactly was so special about this distinct day or this specific man, that the sun and moon were stopped on his behalf enabling him to defeat His enemies the Amorites? I can recall many times when I wished the Lord would have given me half that favor with some of my enemies! In studying this scripture, I greatly pondered what it may have been about this particular incident, that made the Lord move in a such a mighty way that the bible records such an occurrence never previously or thereafter occurred again in history.

The very first thing I understood was that the Lord at one time had wanted the Amorites completely destroyed *(Deuteronomy 20:17)*. Immediately I began to understand that this truly was the Lord's battle. Many times we find ourselves reciting "The battle is not mine, it's the Lord's" but how quickly we can misuse this. You see the Lord provided favor where one was promoting His cause! Yes, many times we get ourselves entangled by our own affairs, and expect the Lord to fight a battle for us which has absolutely nothing to do with Him. As a matter of fact, by asking ourselves one simple question we can gain clarity for many of the situations we find ourselves in; "Did the Lord tell you to do it?" So, if he didn't tell us to go there in the first place why do we now find ourselves whining and complaining about why he isn't rushing to fix it?

We can deceive ourselves into thinking that God is supposed to right our wrongs, but if we take on things which we never consulted him for, and if he immediately delivers us, before we can learn the lesson at hand, then we are apt to make the same mistakes again. Hence, some of the situations we will find ourselves in life can be quite painful, until we learn to walk in the way the Lord leads us in.

We don't have much time left to try and figure things out for ourselves, we must learn obedience. Our steps need to be divinely ordered by him. He directs our footsteps where he plans to sustain us and to the places where he has already made provision. He will keep us in a place of purpose, where He can use us even if it means putting the sun and moon on pause. Joshua did not go into this battle blindly, he heard from the Lord first!

I am not sure what this means to you, but I am surely moved into a deeper faith by just reading this story. By Joshua's command, that the Sun and Moon remain at a stand-still, an entire nation was avenged against its enemies. Notice Joshua never asked God if he would stop the Sun and the Moon, he merely had a confidence that whatever it took, the Lord would surely do His part to fulfill His promise.

Prayer and Meditation Scripture: Do not fear or be dismayed because of this great multitude, for the battle is not yours but God's". (2 Chronicles 20:15

Morning Assignment: Don't miss these two small words "but God's", this is what Joshua understood that we are still struggling to comprehend. God is the same yesterday, today and forever. He did it for Joshua, and He will do it for you! As you take the time to pray and meditate ask the Lord to help you regain your confidence in His promises. Focus for a moment on the amazing power it takes to interrupt the natural course of the sun and the moon, and accept the lengths that God is willing to go through to see His will transpire in your life. There isn't a force that God would not contend against regarding His Beloved.

Evening Journal:

*Reflect on Your Morning Assignment and note what happened today as a result of you trying something new. Write about what you **thought** would happen, what **actually** happened, what you **learned**, and what you would do **differently** the next time.*

A Friend is He

Greater love has no man than to lay down his life for his friend.
John 15:13

Jesus teaches us all about the Agape love of the father and in his unyielding passion for mankind, he lays down his life for all. If he indeed is the example for us all to follow, we must then ask ourselves

"Do we honestly demonstrate a lifestyle which reflects that we have laid down our own desires, and taken up the eternal causes of Christ? Do we reflect HIS love when others act unloving toward us, or when we are not treated how we feel we deserve to be treated? Can we comfortably say that we exemplify the character of Christ?"

I will share with you how the revelation of the above scripture entered my life in a personal way. Early during my Christian walk, I was betrayed by someone very close to me and needless to say very hurt in the process. I believed that because of the nature of the hurt, that it was time to distance myself from this person. While deceived, I believed that I had forgiven them, and just needed distance in order to not leave any open doors for this to occur again. However, the Lord quickly revealed to me that I was walking in offense and that it was a clever trick of the enemy designed to cause division. The Lord asked me plainly to just turn the other cheek. I argued with God, for a brief moment, explaining to him how I felt justified in my decision to end the relationship, how good and sincere of a person I had always been, and that I deserved better. The Lord assured me that he wanted me to walk in complete forgiveness. I knew better than to argue, and although I felt utterly confused, betrayed and abandoned I quietly found myself uttering these very words, "Greater love has no man than to lay down his life for his friend. Jesus I call you friend, I lay down my life in exchange for yours."

I can hardly explain the calming peace I felt at that very moment. My feelings were still very hurt, yet in a place deeper than my feelings was a "knowing" that if I yielded in obedience everything was going to be alright. I had decided to be obedient despite how wronged I was feeling and turned the other cheek, and in exchange it turned out to be one of the most powerful opportunities for me to truly minister the love of God. My Godly inspired response caused this person to take a deep look at themselves. Better yet, I was able to help this person deal with the open doors in their own life that had caused them a history of bad and broken relationships. I could never have imagined what ONE simple act of obedience had the power to do!

I honestly did not understand what the Lord was requiring of me as I was going through this situation, but I later realized that he had entrusted me with this trial not only for them, but also to kill the fleshy responses which had been secretly working behind the scenes of my own life. Although my immediate response would have been to react as everyone else in this persons life had, God, had something much more glorious in mind for us both.

Prayer and Meditation Scripture: Do not repay evil with evil or insult with insult, but with blessing, because to this you were called so that you may inherit a blessing (1 Peter 3:9).

Morning Assignment: Adhering to this command will not always feel good but, the Lord assures us that obedience is well worth the reward. As you move forth today with your usual activities, set your intention to express yourself from a place of obedience and sensitivity to the Holy Spirit. Close your eyes for a few minutes and as you meditate begin to feel yourself responding in a loving manner to someone who might present a challenging situation (we all have them in our lives and they are there for a reason). If you are currently in a situation that is stressful, envision this person or group of persons. Then allow yourself to feel all the emotions of how they presently make you feel and then allow yourself to feel all the options of which you can choose to respond by. Initially,this might be uncomfortable but press ahead with the exercise until you can actually feel the peaceful responses. This power belongs to you, don't let others rob you of it. Be generous with the time you give to this exercise and then ask the Lord to reveal how he'd like for you to respond. During this time have your bible close by so that should he choose to speak through His word you will be ready. If you deliberately seek God, he will offer some pretty creative solutions. You will begin to grow spiritually as you allow yourself to open up to Him and permit yourself to flow in His love. You may find some situations to be particularly challenging, however this is what it truly means to lay downs one's life.

Evening Journal:

*Reflect on Your Morning Assignment and note what happened today as a result of you trying something new. Write about what you **thought** would happen, what **actually** happened, what you **learned**, and what you would do **differently** the next time.*

Transformational Power

And all of us, as with unveiled face, [because we] continued to behold [in the Word of God] as in a mirror the glory of the Lord, are constantly being transfigured into His very own image in ever increasing splendor and from one degree of glory to another; [for this comes] from the Lord [Who is] the Spirit. *1 Peter 2:20*

We behold His glory as in a mirror, being continuously changed until we are reflecting the very image of our creator. How thrilling is the thought that we are entering new realms of existence, in ourselves through him, which will reveal a glory that the world has never known before. I don't know about you, but accepting this truth makes me feel like everything I have ever encountered during this life's journey all becomes worthwhile. Every pain, every trial, every crisis, has a transformational power to bring forth the required change necessary for a greater glory to be revealed in each one of us.

I'm overjoyed and rejoicing at what this means to me personally and pray that you are also gaining a deeper insight and understanding about the issues we face in life, perhaps even a change of mind-set. You see the LORD is teaching us to see His glory during the dark, dismal, and hopeless moments in our lives. He is bringing to light that supernatural provision, healing, and miracles are his plan for our lives, but he manifests this through our faith in Him, during crises moments. Negative faith which is fear, produces negative outcomes, but the supernatural faith of God, now that produces far above what we could ask, think, or imagine!

We must learn during difficult times, to humble ourselves, depend more on Him, and allow Him into our circumstances. The contrary would be to sink into self-pity, regress, and never achieve higher heights. You see there are places in His glory which not all humans will be able to withstand but, the Good News is he allows us by free will to determine how much of His Glory, we want revealed in our lives. Many times we say we want to experience his glory but run in the opposite direction of the things that will bring forth that glory. So essentially we want the glory, without laboring for it. Being transfigured comes from evolving in Him through the fiery trials of affliction.

Prayer and Meditation Scripture: You are my lamp, O LORD; the LORD turns my darkness into light. (2 Samuel 22:29)

Morning Assignment: Take an assessment of all the issues you are presently being challenged with. Begin to list them one by one, and notice how dark, deep and impossible some of those things may seem. Then, set your intention to allow God's light to shine in those situations. Pray and meditate on the above scripture and ask the Lord to reveal the purpose for which these things have been permitted to appeared in your life and the ways in which He desires to overtake the dark areas with His light. It will take willingness and diligence but, remember that it's in our weaknesses that God is made perfect and its in these dark areas that he desires to see His light manifest. His word becomes a mirror for our lives and the longer we abide in His word, the more we are being transfigured into His very own image.

Evening Journal:

*Reflect on Your Morning Assignment and note what happened today as a result of you trying something new. Write about what you **thought** would happen, what **actually** happened, what you **learned**, and what you would do **differently** the next time.*

Knowing the Truth

And you will know the truth, and the truth will set you free.
John 8:32 (ESV)

Knowing, here, refers to intimate knowledge of, not just a general understanding of, but a revelational, transformational, and evidential knowing. Jesus says in (John 14:6) I am the way, the truth, and the life; so in essence, acquiring a true, deep, and close relationship with Christ is the process by which one is set free.

Some reading this may be thinking, but how can I be set free when I am not even bound? The answer lies in understanding that all sin brings along with it some type of bondage, it's the law of sin and death. (The wages of sin is death -Romans 6:23). We were born into sin, by way of Adam, and this sin nature brings along with it a measure of death to different areas of our lives. Jesus, being the second Adam—the one we are re-born from—redeems us from the curse of sin and death. (Who gave himself for us, that he might redeem us from all iniquity, Titus 2:14)

So, in Christ we have the power to overcome, but because sin can go undetected and because of its hidden nature, it can operate in our lives unbeknownst to us through generational curses, unforgivingness, lack of repentance, and all of this causes spiritual blindness. So, how can one tell if they are bound? Take a serious look at your life, identify the areas that maybe lacking or are most broken, the areas that don't have life and growth, but instead have more stagnation, passivity, and laxness. This is a form of death, if it is not growing, then it is dying. Is it financial death—trouble maintaining and managing money? Marital death—in the form of divorce, loneliness, or living in an unfulfilled marriage? Is it emotional or mental instability, or physical illnesses, or addictions? All these, and others, are areas of our lives are left wide open for death to attack and the evidence is in what's manifested. The fact that there is so no growth in them, suggests that something else other than the truth of God's word is present. Something else is operating, and if its not the truth of God's word that is operating, then it is the lies of Satan that are at work! This is exactly what Jesus came to set us free from. *The thief comes only to steal and kill and destroy. I came that they may have life and have it abundantly. (John 10:10)*

So, once we come into the knowledge of truth, we experience freedom from these oppressions. Wherever God's truths are not present, is territory accessible to the enemy. So the truths of God that we know, believe, and implement sets us free...

Freedom, is a state of existence whereby life's occurrences, especially the difficult ones, are all viewed as opportunities to heal, develop, and grow into alignment with the will of God for our lives. This perspective of life allows one to cooperate with the flow of the Holy Spirit within their life and releases their grip of a desired outcome. This is the true hallmark of a spiritually mature person, when God's will is accepted in place of one's own, understanding that it may not always be comfortable or our habitual nature. It is from this place of surrender that one develops an internal harmony that then begins to change the world around them. This stance determines how one engages life, and who they become in it. Think of Jesus in the Garden of Gethsemane, when he was being delivered to the cross, he utters, *"not my will, but your will be done"*. Naturally, he did not want to be crucified, but spiritually, his knowledge of the truth—of him becoming the savior of the world—far outweighed his fear and allowed Him to fulfill God's purpose for His life. He endured temporary discomfort in exchange for His destiny!

> ***Prayer and Meditation Scripture:*** Now the Lord is the Spirit, and where the Spirit of the Lord is, there is freedom. (2 Corinthians 3:17) ESV

Morning Assignment: So, to the degree of which the word of God (His truths), are alive and operating within us, is to the degree of freedom we experience in our lives. As you meditate today, determine to be free to become the highest and greatest expression of your divine self. Begin by accepting your own inner and outer beauty. Become the standard as opposed to being transforming into someone else's standard. Use the word of God as a mirror to reflect upon, and from there you can ask Him to fix whatever He would like to have fixed, embrace the rest, and resolve to walk the pathway that leads to the best you!

Evening Journal:

*Reflect on Your Morning Assignment and note what happened today as a result of you trying something new. Write about what you **thought** would happen, what **actually** happened, what you **learned**, and what you would do **differently** the next time.*

Out of Darkness, Into the Light

Who hath delivered us from the power of darkness, and hath translated us into the kingdom of his dear Son: Colossians 1:13

The Kingdom of Darkness, is a dimension consisting of every type of evil, ignorance, and oppression. Through oppression and fear the enemy has built his kingdom and has insidiously carried out his mission statement to steal, kill and destroy. Great destinies have been aborted, annointed men and women of God have fallen, and many have been robbed of the opportunities to fulfill God's intended outcome for their lives. Since the enemy has had much time to perfect the powers of darkness, we can become easily beguiled by his lies and deception. Notwithstanding, the Kingdom of God has a much greater power at work within each and every one of us.

When we have bought into the lies of the enemy, a subtle paralysis and passivity begins to encroach upon our mind sets and we gradually falter into indifference. Here is where the enemy sets up camp, because indifference makes the way for doubt and unbelief. We then begin to rationalize and justify our actions and build upon these limiting belief systems until we become victims of our own self-made prisons. Some of us have build such elaborate fortresses and high-security confinements, that the vicious guard dogs called defense and avoidance mechanisms set out to devour anyone who comes too close. We hurt those that come into our lives to help us, we live life in repeat self-abuse cycles, and we never really get a breakthrough. All the while, we portray an illusive image of having it together, being stable and being comfortable with ourselves, when in fact we are trapped!

Yes, we may know to claim Christianity, claim redemption, and to pray, but we fail miserably to get passed the deceptions the enemy sets up from within. The enemy has stalwart plans to deceive us into a perpetual paralytic state of repetitive monotony. Wasting the years, void of any true signs of progression within our lives .

Ironically, most of us get into this deceived state by being busy. Yes, we are deceived into believing that by ability and strength and sometimes even anointing, we are creating our own destinies. There couldn't be a greater deception than this. The word reminds us that *"many are the plans of man, but it is the purposes of God which prevail"* Proverbs 19:21.

Prayer and Meditation Scripture: And set your minds and keep them set on what is above (the higher things), not on the things that are on the earth. Colossians 3:2 (AMP)

Morning Assignment: Most of humanity operates through oppressive fears which are based on limited belief systems. We limit God, and we already know somewhere deep inside that we are limited without Him. You see what we think we believe and what really believe aren't always the same thing. What we really believe has an interesting way of showing up in our lives. It sometimes shows up as trials, confusion, depression, sickness, unhappiness, and despair. These are warnings that something isn't quite right from within. So to change what exists around us, we must first change what exists within us. The enemy will fight you in the area of your mind with all kinds of ungodly, evil, and hateful thoughts toward yourself and toward others, when you are being delivered into the Kingdom of Light. **You must resist coming into agreement or being enticed by these thoughts.** At times, it may take for you to declare out loud that you will only submit to holy thoughts and the Holy Spirit. We must resolve to not be dragged back into the dark Kingdom we've been delivered from. As you mediate today, disconnect from every negative or limited belief about yourself and others, set your mind and keep it set on things above, this is how we gain access to the higher realms of understanding. *Therefore, as God's chosen people, holy and dearly loved, clothe yourselves with compassion, kindness, humility, gentleness, and patience. Bear with each other and forgive one another if any of you has a grievance against someone. Forgive as the Lord forgave you. And over all these virtues put on love, which binds them all together in perfect unity. Let the peace of Christ rule in your hearts, -Colossians 3:12-15.*

Evening Journal:

*Reflect on Your Morning Assignment and note what happened today as a result of you trying something new. Write about what you **thought** would happen, what **actually** happened, what you **learned**, and what you would do **differently** the next time.*

Releasing Offense

A person's wisdom makes him slow to anger, and it is his glory to overlook an offense. Proverbs 19:11

How many have ever had a conversation with someone, and what you "heard" them say and what they "really" said were two different things? I have encountered people being offended by something that they presumed had been said, done, or intended which had nothing to do with what actually happened. I am often bewildered as to how quickly one would jump to their own conclusions or listen to only half a matter, rather than thoroughly search the matter out.

Misunderstandings, probably lead to more offenses than anything else. So offenses don't only come by way of someone actually being mistreated, they also come by way of someone believing whole-heartedly that they have been treated unjustly, regardless of how distorted their facts may be. The prince of the power of the air is very real, and is always seeking an opportunity to inject his wickedness somewhere in the atmosphere that exists between what one person speaks and what the other person hears. That empty space in between is really not empty space at all. Understanding this, we can gain an edge over the demonic by utilizing the fruit of the spirit to engage. You see, no one is ever offended by loving, gentle, and kind interactions. My point being, that one can effectively get their point across and still be non-offensive.

God is concerned with how we handle people and situations. Both parties have a requirement, the offender to learn a better approach, and the offended to release the occasion and wash it with forgiveness and grace. The longer we allow an offense to continue, the more deeply rooted it becomes. Prolonged festering and replaying of the event or words spoken, eventually gives rise to bitterness. It is our inherent human inclination to want to hold on to an offense, so we must be willing to allow the Holy Spirit to complete this work in us and teach us how to forgive and let things go.

Now take a moment to be honest with yourself, are you handling offenses as scripture instructs? Think on this: How can we feel justified harboring an offense against someone, if we cannot our own selves do what the word advises? Isn't that hypocritical in nature? Doesn't that fact that we hold on to the offense make us just as sinful as the one doing the offending?

So how exactly do we overlook an offense, when we truly feel we have been wronged? It is helpful to first put it in God's hands by letting go of any associated emotions. Each time you say *I felt* or *I felt as if,* you are operating from the emotional realm within the soul. God desires instead we be led by the spirit, His spirit, which is His truths. Meaning despite how you may feel about it, you decide to do as His word commands.

Let's review a few scriptures regarding this: *A brother offended is more unyielding than a strong city, and quarreling is like the bars of a castle.* (Proverbs 18:19) *Good sense makes one slow to anger, and it is his glory to overlook an offense.* (Proverbs 19:11) *Do not take to heart all the things that people say, lest you hear your servant cursing you. Your heart knows that many times you yourself have cursed others.* (Ecclesiastes 7:21-22) ESV

Secondly, look past the offense and discern the need. Discern what is really operating behind the others persons behavior, and adjust your responses accordingly, this can shift what would otherwise be an evil ploy of division and discord and alternately bring glory to God's kingdom. Remember, the Lord desires that there be no divisions among us as fellow believers.

> ***Prayer and Meditation Scripture:*** Great peace have they which love thy law: and nothing shall offend them. (Psalm 119:165)

Morning Assignment: As you pray and meditate on the above scripture, begin setting your intention upon **your response** to offenses. It does not mean you become a doormat for offenses, it means you learn how to handle them maturely and wisely. Pray for patience, and the other fruit of the spirit (according to Galatians 5:22), and throughout the day look for opportunities to express those characteristics. Ask the Lord to guide you in how to see the need or weakness in other people. Once you are able to realize that need and act upon it, you can then turn the situation around. It takes much practice and much patience, but once you learn to do this, you will become a vessel that can be powerfully used in the battlefield.

While you are doing this exercise, begin to journal your experiences in handling offenses. Take as many days as you need on this exercise, and be willing to do it until something changes. When you take the time to deliberately focus on you and your responses, and decide to align yourself with God's word and His will, you will encounter a new, improved, and more empowered you!

Evening Journal:

Reflect on Your Morning Assignment and note what happened today as a result of you trying something new. Write about what you **thought** would happen, what **actually** happened, what you **learned**, and what you would do **differently** the next time.

Jealous Roots

And it came to pass as they came, when David was returned from the slaughter of the Philistine, that the women came out of all cities of Israel, singing and dancing, to meet king Saul, with tabrets, with joy, and with instruments of musick. And the women answered one another as they played, and said, Saul hath slain his thousands, and David his ten thousands. And Saul was very wroth, and the saying displeased him; and he said, They have ascribed unto David ten thousands, and to me they have ascribed but thousands: and what can he have more but the kingdom? And Saul eyed David from that day and forward.

1 Samuel 18:6-9

There is enough greatness in God, for each soul to evolve to its fullest potential without being a threat to the livelihood of anyone else. We can gather from the scriptural text, that this ONE incident was the seed of Saul's rankling jealousy, continual obsession, and dreadful threat of David's righteous promotion. When the Lord decides to elevate and promote someone himself, it's not rare to see those in superior positions and those in their midst perceive this good thing as somehow threatening. In fact, I personally believe this is why promotions in life come with a change of network, your circle of people changes to rise up to the new level being afforded to you. I'm not speaking of a corporate promotion of a higher title and bigger pay, I'm referring to spiritual promotion, expressing your authentic nature, when all you do comes up prosperous because you've elevated your beliefs.

While David's victory here was indeed a good thing for both Saul and the entire nation of Israel, Saul's twisted distortion of reality did not allow him to benefit from the blessing the Lord was giving him. This story noted to be a favorite amongst many Christians, clearly depicts what happens to us when we fuel jealousy with fear, suspicion, and false perceptions. We see at the end of this story how this one seed blossoms into a full blown alienation from God and ultimately brings King Saul to his own demise.

Herein lies the issue; when all you see is the comparison between yourself and others and are unable to accept God's favor on them, you rob yourself of the blessing which God intends for you to have. This is when it's time for self-examination and repentance; delusions of grandeur are not far away--don't fall into this trap. 2 Thessalonians 2:9-12 warns us that the Lord will send a spirit of delusion to condemn those who have not believed the truth but have delighted in wickedness.

Perception is everything. Let's briefly explore the angle of natural human emotions. When we experience jealousy, we feel a range of uncomfortable emotions including inferiority, inadequacy, and often times even anger and resentment. These feelings of discomfort can serve a greater purpose once you learn to recognize them as internal warning signs. During those times, instead of giving into those feelings and harboring them negatively against the individual or circumstance that made you feel this way, realize instead that you are having an encounter with a portion of yourself reflected through that individual, and the reason it makes you uncomfortable is because you have now identified your own potential, you just haven't learned yet how to materialize it in your own life. Their accomplishments mirror what you are capable of, but not yet knowledgeable of.

Jealousy is a human emotion that we will all inevitably face in life. What we do when we experience these feelings, however determines where we end up. Understand, that we are most vulnerable to jealousies when we are in unstable relationships or at any major point of transition in life. These places leave us feeling vulnerable and one of the most powerful things to do during these times is to bless any person you maybe feeling that way towards. You can send them encouragement or compliments, you can pray for them, you can volunteer to help them, or simply give them a gift. This one principle has such a powerful impact in the realm of the spirit.

> ***Prayer and Meditation Scripture:*** For where envying and strife is, there is confusion and every evil work (James 3:16).

Morning Assignment: As you pray and meditate on the above scripture ask the Lord to reveal areas whereby you may have hidden envies or jealousies operating. Be willing to confess them to the Lord. Be willing to explain to Him why you feel this way. Once you set your intention to be healed in this area, ask the Lord to show you ways in which you can be a greater expression of peace, harmony, and unity rather than competitiveness and divisiveness. Once you are able to see the truth of what is operating its much easier to separate yourself from those thoughts. Journal these experiences to quickly help you grow in this area and later help you more easily identify when jealousies and envies are working in yourself and in others. Don't let these feelings linger around lest they become bitter roots.

Evening Journal:

*Reflect on Your Morning Assignment and note what happened today as a result of you trying something new. Write about what you **thought** would happen, what **actually** happened, what you **learned**, and what you would do **differently** the next time.*

Letting Go

Then Peter came to Jesus and asked, "Lord, how many times shall I forgive my brother or sister who sins against me? Up to seven times?" Jesus answered, "I tell you, not seven times, but seventy-seven times".
                                        Matthew 18:21-22

What exactly is forgiveness and how will I know when I have truly forgiven? Forgiveness, in short, is releasing the negative emotions we associate to a past experience in order to facilitate positive change for our future. I know that may sound like a mouthful but, if we can grasp that our current perception of past negative experiences has the capacity to affect our future either adversely or favorably, then we are better able to adapt a healthier mind-set as it relates to our life experiences.

Although I used the word perceived [perception], this is not to lessen or invalidate any of our experiences, it serves instead to help us move forward in spite of how horrible our experiences may have been. So, what am I saying? If we can fathom that everything we have experienced is helping to shape who we are to become, we can begin to embrace that sometimes things happen to us which can ultimately be used for a greater purpose. It creates within us a compassion for others we would otherwise not have. It reveals to us how we can endure things we thought we would never be able to. It opens up our eyes to understanding life from a different but healthier viewpoint.

How long will you stay hurt and angry? We will never make others suffer as a result of holding onto a hurt they may have caused, but rather we give them power over us by cleaving on to the negative feelings we associate to them. Feelings of hate, guilt, shame, animosity, regret and resentment, don't serve any beneficial purpose in our lives and should therefore not be occupying any space in our heart. Whatever we decide to hold on to in our hearts, appears in our lives. So if its negative, expect it will show up!

Most people believe that when you forgive someone, you are somehow permitting the person to hurt you again; that's a false belief that serves to keep you guarded. You must be willing to outgrow that temporary "safe behavior" and step into a more mature state of accepting what you cannot change; making peace with the perpetrator(s) and with yourself. As long as you hold on to what is useless, there isn't enough room in your heart to receive God's best. If you long to experience wholeness of life, you must first have wholeness of heart. You will never possess in life what does not first reside deep in your heart. So, when the only thing you remember about an individual is what they did to you, it's time to forgive.

When we are cleansed from the past and don't allow what happened yesterday to rule our lives today, we destroy the grip it has on us and we are therefore free to live and love authentically. With that being said, let's never forget that in this world, one way or another, we will all inevitably experience hurt and sometimes hurt others, however, we hold the power to forgive and ask for forgiveness.

Prayer and Meditation Scripture: For if you forgive others their trespasses, your heavenly Father will also forgive you (Matthew 6:14).

Morning Assignment: When we apply the scripture to forgive not only seven offenses but seventy-seven instead, we are reminded that forgiveness is then a way of life, and not a one-time decision. As you move forth today, set your intention to accepting this truth. As you pray and meditate on the above scripture begin asking the Lord to reveal persons of which you may be harboring unforgivingness towards. Once the Lord brings their names and/or faces to your mind begin to release whatever negative emotions you feel residing in your body. Be deliberate and command those feelings to leave your body, mind, soul and heart. Then replace them by radiating feelings of love towards them, this may be especially difficult for someone who has hurt or violated you, but ask the Lord for His help. He will help. Remember he is a very present help in the time of need, we need just ask and believe. Once again, it may take repeating this exercise several times, but be willing to do it until you feel the release. Once you begin to see your past in a healthier light, you can express a healthier more authentic you in the present.

Evening Journal:

*Reflect on Your Morning Assignment and note what happened today as a result of you trying something new. Write about what you **thought** would happen, what **actually** happened, what you **learned**, and what you would do **differently** the next time.*

Are you Filled?

But ye shall receive power, after that the Holy Ghost is come upon you: and ye shall be witnesses unto me both in Jerusalem, and in all Judaea, and in Samaria, and unto the uttermost part of the earth. Acts 1:8

How will people know if they are filled with His Spirit? To be filled means to fully take on the character of Christ and the ability to not only walk in miracles, signs, and wonders as did Christ, but in His own words "*performing even greater works than these*". The reason we aren't seeing this type of power evident in our lives today is because many simply are not filled. A person who is truly filled with the Holy Spirit does not lie, cheat, steal, or do anything that the Holy Spirit does not lead him or her to do. Great people in the bible did extraordinary things because they were able to yield to the direction and instruction of the Holy Spirit that lived on the inside of them and filled them.

What kind of witness are we being if we are not filled? We are either credible or non-credible witnesses. Talking in tongues, does not mean we are filled; our character denotes whether we are filled, and where there is still room for ungodly things to operate, then we are not corroborating with the type of witness He has called us to be. So how do we become the type of Spirit filled, fully empowered, witnesses that he mentions in the scripture above? By yielding completely to the leading of the Holy Spirt.

A self-directed life, is at the root of all defeat. Self-focus dethrones Christ as the center of our lives and does not permit our steps to be guided by him, so the path we end up on is limited, defeated, and powerless.

It is impossible to walk dynamically in the Spirit without spending time in fellowship with our Lord in His word, in prayer, and in personal study. We must listen attentively to Him for His direction in our daily activities and then we can witness for Christ powerfully. True followers of Christ listen and obey out of love and a reverential fear of Him.

One of the greatest acts of obedience is to share Christ with others in the power of the Holy Spirit. This means we demonstrate His power and others identify it.

The Body of Christ must come into full maturity in Him. He desires His will to be done all of the time, through those who are willing to follow Him out of holiness and a great love for Him. This depth of love and holiness can only be given to you by walking as close to Him as I have shared with you. Are you willing to do this for Him?

Prayer and Meditation Scripture: With great power the apostles continued to testify to the resurrection of the Lord Jesus. And God's grace was so powerfully at work in them all. (Acts 4:33)

Morning Assignment: As you move forth today set your intention to demonstrate the power of the Holy Spirit at His will. This power does not come from you but works through you as you submit yourself fully to the spirit of God and obey what He asks of you. The more you surrender to His will, the more strongly you will be able to demonstrate his power, the stronger you demonstrate his power, the more powerful of a witness you will be. Close your eyes, and as you begin to pray and meditate on the above scripture, ask for a greater sensitivity to the Holy Spirits leading in all matters.

Center and still yourself from within to hear what the Lord is saying to you. Then once you hear the instructions, follow through in obedience and watch God's will flow in your life in ways that will amaze, astonish and influence others producing a most powerful testimony. As you journal in the evening remember to list any struggles you may have encountered during this exercise. This will enable you to focus more clearly on any hindrances and allow you to grow in greater sensitivity to the Holy Spirit's leading.

Evening Journal:

*Reflect on Your Morning Assignment and note what happened today as a result of you trying something new. Write about what you **thought** would happen, what **actually** happened, what you **learned**, and what you would do **differently** the next time.*

Which Right is Wrong?

There is a way which seemeth right unto a man, but the end thereof are the ways of death. Proverbs 14:12

There will inevitably be times in our lives where we will be faced with pressing decisions. We will ponder upon these for prolonged periods of time, we will ask friends and family for advice, or we may pray for guidance. During these times, it is critical that Christians understand their vulnerability to demonic influence. We can easily be misled to believe that there isn't much to lose, and that some small decisions may seem trivial or unimportant. But let me remind you that we must acknowledge the Lord in ALL our ways. Because the Lord is exposing here that there are two rights—there is the right when you are being led by your soul and there is the right when you are being led by His spirit. Spirit begets spirit, flesh begets flesh.

When you experience confusion, these two are at war. Confusion is the by-product of your soul and your spirit battling for an intended outcome. See, Satan has a desire for you *"And the Lord said, Simon, Simon, behold, Satan hath desired to have you, that he may sift you as wheat"* Luke 22:31-32. We are in a winnable war against the defeated kingdom of darkness; but the lies of Satan can gain a measure of control in our lives if we believe them. Conversely, the Lord also has desires for you *"Beloved, I wish above all things that you may prosper and be in health, even as your soul prospers."* 3 John 1:2

When we experience confusion about making righteous decisions, we are usually being called to face a fear that has been insidiously operating in our lives. The soul does not want to feel pain, rejection, or failure. The Holy Spirit is telling us don't believe the lie, that is not my plan for you! How much trauma or abuse a person associates with these feelings, determines their ability to differentiate between what is of the Holy Spirit and what is of the flesh. This is a tricky place for us all and it is at these times when we must surrender our pain, will, and desires in exchange for something greater to lead our lives. This is the place where self-abuse cycles are broken. When we continue to make decisions out of our wounded-ness, this is the Right which is Wrong. This is where the enemy wants to keep you.

Satan prepares many deceitful temptations to lure the people of God from His destiny for them. Most of the times when he is successful it's because he uses our past wounds; things we have not yet been healed and delivered from. These wounds cause spiritual blindness and so we are not able to see what is operating in our lives and governing our decisions. We then begin to reason and rationalize wrong decisions and motives and feel justified explaining them, this is the very nature of a sinful heart. This is the primary reason why we need strong spiritual leaders in our lives. Leaders that can reach us, who genuinely care for our well-being and who are not afraid to tell us what we need to hear.

The purpose of being spirit-led is that the mind of your spirit, (which is the mind of Christ) can now make decisions beyond the wounds and hurts. The point of submitting all things to Him is for our benefit, not His. Trust me, we are doing God no favors. Simply put, it is His unwavering love and compassion through His undying grace and mercy whereby He affords us this opportunity. What we do with it is up to us.

Prayer and Meditation Scripture: The way of fools seems right to them, but the wise listen to advice (Proverbs 12:15).

Morning Assignment: As you move forth today, set your intention to seek advice from God regarding all your decisions. As you pray and meditate on the above scripture ask the Holy Spirit to be your wise council. List some decisions you must make which you would normally seek the advice of others, or which you would just make on your own, and offer them to God for his advice and direction. The Lord loves speaking to us in different ways so that we don't become complacent in our walk with him. Open yourself up to receive in which ever manner he decides to speak and then make sure you follow through. As you move throughout the day listen to the different ways in which he may be answering you and journal them. You will know its Him because the answer will resonate from a deep place within you. Remember to always honor the still small voice on the inside, it may not immediately give you the answer, but it will always guide you towards it.

Evening Journal:

*Reflect on Your Morning Assignment and note what happened today as a result of you trying something new. Write about what you **thought** would happen, what **actually** happened, what you **learned**, and what you would do **differently** the next time.*

"Christ-Like" Love

"And now these three remain: faith, hope and love. But the greatest of these is love," (1 Corinthians 13:13)

Do we really know what genuine love is? When we possess the love of God we have no problem doing right by those who hate us, hurt us, and use us. This kind of love is the power that Jesus Christ walked in. Although difficult to accomplish, with the guiding power of the Holy Ghost, it is possible! God's supernatural love differs from ours. Let's take a look at when Jesus was washing the feet of His disciples, a powerful demonstration of the God type love in action.

In John chapter 13, Jesus takes a moment to explain to his disciples, that although they would not comprehend what He was doing, they would eventually come into a full understanding. You see, The Lord Jesus already knew who was going to betray Him and that was why He goes on to say, *"And you are clean, though not every one of you." (John 13:10)*. Pause, right there! Jesus was staring pure evil right in its face, the kind of evil that would eventually deliver Him to the place of His crucifixion experience, the worst evil and human brutality in the history of all mankind. Yet, He chooses NOT to provoke a fight or argument with Judas nor does He give him a piece of His mind. Instead He humbles Himself into a lowly position to wash the feet of His perpetrator. Can we honestly say that we possess this kind of love? Jesus knew something that more often than not, Christians tend to ignore—God the father is directly involved in all of our affairs. God allowed the enemy to do all that he would do and then God had His turn. Jesus didn't put up resistance or go into denial they way many of us do. No, he set His intention upon eternal things and with boldness of heart, he allowed God to have the final victory by demonstrating untainted humility in the face of adversity. Nothing that the enemy could do to Him would ever top the glorious resurrection that came after the cross!

I can assuredly say that, most true believers, to one degree or another, have had similar face-offs with this type of evil, but it's what we decide to do in these moments, which ultimately determines our fate. When we take matters into our own hands and decide not to confer with God, He, in turn, leaves us to deal with the consequences of our own decisions.

Jesus indeed demonstrated the unconditional, agape love of the Father. In fact, just a little later in verse 34 (John 13:34) He reiterates this point by stating, *"A new commandment I give unto you, that ye love one another; as I have loved you"*. He is not speaking of love the way we may feel like giving it—conditionally, but rather the manner of love in which He loved us "while we were yet sinners", just like Judas. So in essence, He sets a standard for Christians, raises the bar, and teaches us to remove all of the conditions by which we love.

> ***Prayer and Meditation Scripture:*** By this shall all men know that ye are my disciples, if ye have love one to another. (John 13:35)

Morning Assignment: So, not only is a new paradigm required to love others how God loves us, but Jesus also says that it will be the signature hallmark which defines that we belong to Him. From this we can safely conclude that a call to His ministry is a call to minister His agape love. As you move forth today, set your intention to demonstrate the love of God to a dark and hurting world: loving the unlovable, excusing the inexcusable, and forgiving the unforgiveable. Christ is not asking us to do something He has not already done Himself. Pray and meditate on the above scripture and ask the Lord to show you where you might have fallen short of demonstrating His love.

Begin to realize that many relationship crises are self-induced dramas based on our refusal to love beyond our preset conditions. Ask the Lord to create new opportunities, starting today, in which you can love beyond the usual. Folks might hate you, use you, talk about you, and betray you, but decide to love them anyway. Remember Judas' betrayal promoted Jesus to the place of eternal victory; to the point that His name is now above every other name! Make up your mind to walk in the standard set above and allow God to take care of the rest.

Evening Journal:

*Reflect on Your Morning Assignment and note what happened today as a result of you trying something new. Write about what you **thought** would happen, what **actually** happened, what you **learned**, and what you would do **differently** the next time.*

A Little Leaven

Ye did run well; who did hinder you that ye should not obey the truth? This persuasion cometh not of Him that calleth you. A little leaven leaveneth the whole lump. Galatians 5:7-9

You may be asking what exactly is leaven? According to dictionary.com leaven is defined as: 1. A substance, as yeast or baking powder, that causes fermentation and expansion of dough or batter. 2. An element that produces an altering or transforming influence.

In both definitions we can deduce that leaven is an element or ingredient that has an effect on the final or end product. So, from a spiritual stance, leaven symbolizes those things in our lives that are affecting its outcome or what has manifested thus far. Paul is teaching the Galatians that You can't include a little sin in your life without it affecting its entire course. *"Who did hinder you that ye should not obey the truth?"*.

I love the way the Epistle of James explains this principle, because James, who was Jesus's oldest half-brother and who so intently understood the dynamics and intricate nature of spiritual warfare, writes in *James 2:10 For whosoever shall keep the whole law, and yet offend in ONE point, he is guilty of ALL. (KJV) (emphasis added, mine)*

A common mistake some Christians make when trying to adhere to this teaching is trying to obtain perfection. You cannot do this on your own and perfection is not the goal. Brokenness and humility before God is the goal. If we have the foundation wrong then it is not a solid place to build upon. Truth is, we all are going to make mistakes, that's why His grace is sufficient. However, what is not OK is to rationalize and argue excuses for sin; we must foster a lifestyle of continual repentance which in turn develops a reliance on God and not ourselves. Believe that a little sin, left unacknowledged, is a little leaven that can ruin the entire lump.

We can safely say then that the purpose of sin is to interfere with God's final product. The work he is doing in and through you. Sin, left unchecked, ignored, or justified can be detrimental to someone who is truly seeking to see God's will and power unfold in their lives.

The last super occurred during the Festival of Unleavened Bread, symbolically this is the reason why during Holy Communion we inwardly examine and judge our lives, not just our sins, but more importantly our overall posture and willingness towards biblical commandments and righteous living.

Our greatest victory comes to us when we can begin to identify the sin operating in our own lives, confess it, repent from it, and be delivered from it. This means what we once struggled with no longer has a hold of our lives. If there is bad manifestation or fruit in your life, then there is leaven in your life. Sin begins at the heart level, your strongest desires and beliefs. However, the first step to identifying sin is not always simple, sin can have a hidden and covert nature to it, meaning its not always easily detectable. This is why reading the word daily, and keeping it in your heart, will help you along the journey. As the heart and mind of God are revealed to you, you will begin to see with an enlightened understanding that which is opposed to God and is affecting the outcome of your own life.

Prayer and Meditation Scripture: Therefore let us keep the feast, not with old leaven, neither with the leaven of malice and wickedness; but with the unleavened bread of sincerity and truth. (1 Corinthians 5:8)

Morning Assignment: Today, as you meditate on the above scripture, ask the Lord to strengthen you in the areas of your life that have sin, lack, or disease operating. It is not God's desire for us to be powerless over these situations, but he desires that we house the anointing that breaks every yoke of sin and bondage and walk in the power that he has given us over all the power of the enemy through Christ. When the temptation to do wrong shows up today, rely on the Holy Spirit to strengthen you. The Bible teaches us *we have not because we ask not* (James 4:2), so when the opportunity presents itself, we merely need to ask the Holy Spirit for help and guidance knowing and believing that he has a great plan for us. *"Then you will call upon Me and come and pray to Me, and I will listen to you.... (Jeremiah 29:12)*

Evening Journaling:

Reflect on Your Morning Assignment and Note what happened today as a result of you trying something new, write about what you thought would happen, what actually happened, what you learned, and what you would do differently the next time.

The Father's Will

"Why do you call me 'Lord, Lord,' and not do what I tell you?
Luke 6:46 ESV

Sad to say, but many professing Christians today are walking around with a false assurance of their salvation in Christ. Jesus spent much time warning us about the attributes of the true versus the false believer. There have been several phases and movements from within the household of faith which have clearly moved away from Christ's requirement for us to enter into heaven. Let's take a closer look at what Jesus himself teaches:

21 "Not everyone who says to me, 'Lord, Lord,' will enter the kingdom of heaven, but only the one who does the will of my Father who is in heaven. 22 Many will say to me on that day, 'Lord, Lord, did we not prophesy in your name and in your name drive out demons and in your name perform many miracles?' 23 Then I will tell them plainly, 'I never knew you. Away from me, you evildoers!'

Jesus describes a certain work that these people believed they were performing, which had nothing to do with the true work of the Kingdom of God. He calls them evil doers and in another translation workers of iniquity. These false teachers and false converts mentioned above have more faith in the power of their own words and in their spiritual gifts than they do in believing & obeying God's word. These are people who would rather look like they are doing the right thing, as opposed to paying the price of sacrifice in true righteousness. Those who have a form of Godliness, but whom He clearly states are not interested in doing the will of the father.

We cannot live like the devil and claim to belong to Christ, if we are disciples of Christ, we must walk like Christ and strive to live a Holy and disciplined life.

I have had several encounters where someone would want to explain to me how they feel about a particular situation and what their personal beliefs on the matter on, but Jesus teaches us that if how you feel and believe on a matter does not line up with the word of God, then you are in danger of being deceived.

Prayer and Meditation Scripture: Do not merely listen to the word, and so deceive yourselves. <u>Do what it says.</u> (James 1:22) NIV

Morning Assignment: If you claim to Love the father , then it's not possible to love him outside of His own word. Although many will want to twist the word or the understanding of the word for their own selfish motives, there is a dying to the self that must take place to truly walk with the Lord. When you are willing to crucify the flesh and its sin nature, then you are in the DO that Jesus is referencing. I did not say that it was easy to do this, but it is possible. I have never known God to deny anyone help who was willing to put their struggles at his feet, and allow Him to deliver them. As you meditate today, begin to inquire of the Lord as to what He would have you to do differently today, what are the habits that he wants you to eradicate, and which are the new behaviors he will have you to implement? Then begin to stretch yourself in those areas as much as possible, just a small step in the right direction daily can be an enormous leap by the end of the week and more so multiplied by the end of the month and the year. The new creature flourishes when we are not mere hearers but doers of the word!

Evening Journal:

*Reflect on Your Morning Assignment and note what happened today as a result of you trying something new. Write about what you **thought** would happen, what **actually** happened, what you **learned**, and what you would do **differently** the next time.*

Fear Not!

"So do not fear, for I am with you; do not be dismayed, for I am your God. I will strengthen you and help you; I will uphold you with my righteous right hand"
(Isaiah 41:10).

Do you create negative mental scenarios that may or may not happen and then convince yourself that they will happen? Do you tend to predict negative outcomes more than positives one when faced with uncertainty? Do you worry or ponder over imagined "what-if" scenarios? All of these are fear based thought processes and can lead to a very unfulfilled and unhappy life.

Where do these fears begin? They begin in our minds. We all conduct a continuous internal dialogue with ourselves. This self-talk then directly affects our emotions, behaviors, and ultimately guides our decisions. The demonic operates in this realm and can influence us greatly if we are not aware. We can tell ourselves things which don't line up with reality, or things that contradict the truth of God's Word. These untruths and destructive self-talks are prime breeding ground for unhealthy behavior patterns. For example, when feelings of discomfort appear, we find ways of not experiencing them. We may go to many extremes to not feel the discomfort, to the point it begins to create a hindrance to that area of our life. This is called avoidance. Avoidance is a simple way of coping by not having to cope. In order to get past this block, we need to replace the untruth with a scriptural truth: "I can cope with any situation in my life with God's strength working through me" (Philippians 4:13). Believing this truth now allows us to boldly step into areas which we would normally avoid. These uncharted areas are where the fulfillment of life lies; these are the arenas of things that we long for but do not believe enough in ourselves to obtain. Our love for God and belief in his word breaks the chains and fetters that keep us bound from achieving success in any of those areas.

The Word of God, is so powerful because this is the very thing which it exposes. His word makes us reflect until we can identify the irrational thinking working in the backdrop our lives. When we have identified that fear is operating, it is time to tell ourselves the truth and release those old beliefs. Be mindful that if you continue to embrace those false beliefs instead of God's truth, you will continue to experience lack in that area of your life. The choice is yours; remember he gives us all free will.

Trusting in God's truths is our ultimate remedy for fear. Yet, that sometimes seems easier said than done. Confronting your fears means exposing yourself to the very thing, person, or situation that is causing that fear to exist in the first place. The finished work on the cross is our assurance that we can expose ourselves without the fear of being defeated. Exposure can be immediate or gradual, in full or in partial doses. Meaning we can use the most user friendly approach that works for us individually, and we can take all the time we need. Honor yourself enough to acknowledge that what might work for someone else may not necessarily work for you. So use the approach that is best for you. The key is exposing yourself to the object of your fear until you no longer fear it, knowing who is there with you.

Prayer and Meditation Scripture: But even if you should suffer for what is right, you are blessed. "Do not fear their threats; do not be frightened." (1 Peter 3:14)

Morning Assignment: Overcoming fear requires an identification and acceptance of what fears are actually there. As you pray and meditate on the scripture above, realize that the Lord desires to grow you in the areas of your life which are presently experiencing stagnation. Seek his guidance for how to begin to grow in those areas and what He desires to see happening in your life, specifically in the fear bound area. Be willing to be stretched, made uncomfortable, and then stretched some more, all the while, *Fear Not!*

Evening Journal:

*Reflect on Your Morning Assignment and note what happened today as a result of you trying something new. Write about what you **thought** would happen, what **actually** happened, what you **learned**, and what you would do **differently** the next time.*

Figuring the Pay Off

I am crucified with Christ: nevertheless I live; yet not I, but Christ liveth in me: and the life which I now live in the flesh I live by the faith of the Son of God, who loved me, and gave himself for me. Galatians 2:20

The price which was paid on calvary far exceeds the total amount of what all global economies put together would ever equate to. Yes, if you calculated the sum total of the entire global economic valuation, you could not amass the price for what the Lord did for us on that day. On that day he made an investment in you and I that would reap a reward greater than anything money could ever buy. This exceedingly great reward is God himself. "I am your exceeding great reward" Genesis 15:1.

God Himself is His people's reward! We can get many things right and miss this one crucial thing. Paul said it well here,"It is no longer I but Christ who liveth in me". Paul understood that the final resting place of God would be in a realm that exists within us. God made a deposit in humanity which was paid for on the cross. What the scripture is defining here for us is the permanent death of our desire to become anything different than God's original plan for us. God's desire is that He be made manifest in all our daily interactions and transactions, "I will walk among you and be your God, and you shall be My people." Leviticus 26:12

There are times when I feel that I am so close to walking in this, when all of a sudden a situation arises and I find myself, not doing what Jesus would do! These times apprise me of things that exist deep inside which the Lord wants to die. There must be a death. *"Nevertheless I tell you the truth; It is expedient for you that I go away: for if I go not away, the Comforter will not come unto you; but if I depart, I will send him unto you." John 16:7*

The comforter is the holy spirit and Gods actionable plan to abide within His people. Jesus makes it all possible; he dies and the dispensation of the Holy Spirit begins. To be filled with His spirit however means that there is room for nothing else. That's the exchange, we exchange all we are for all HE is. I'm not sure about you but that surely sounds like a win-win to me.

The awesome thing about redemption is that the Lord himself will clean us and wash away the impurities, we don't have to do it alone, we must be willing for him to do it in and through us.

The industry of "Self" is shrinking in these end-times. When you figure the pay off, and calculate the ROI (Return On Investment) is the lord benefiting from His investment in you? Meaning He sacrificed His only son so that we might be saved and live empowered. Does your life reflect one of salvation and empowerment?

Prayer and Meditation Scripture: Ye are bought with a price; be not ye the servants of men (1 Corinthians 7:23)

Morning Assignment: As you pray and meditate on the scripture above, realize that we were bought with a price to be free. If we are not fully free then we are bound. Bondage comes in many forms and we will never be freed from the things we don't even acknowledge or realize are operating in our lives. Satan would love to keep you lacking in your life, but the Lord desires you be prosperous and successful in every area. **Ask the Lord to reveal which things are causing hindrances in your life, confess them before him, renounce them, and repent from them.** A lifestyle of willingness will yield a great payoff in the end.

Evening Journal:

*Reflect on Your Morning Assignment and note what happened today as a result of you trying something new. Write about what you **thought** would happen, what **actually** happened, what you **learned**, and what you would do **differently** the next time.*

Release the Anointing

And thou shalt put them upon Aaron thy brother, and his sons with him; and shalt anoint them, and consecrate them, and sanctify them, that they may minister unto me in the priest's office. Exodus 28:41

During this time, The Lord was safeguarding the worship of the temple by giving strict adherence to the priesthood regarding their duties and roles. He was clearly delineating the roles of the priesthood to guard Israel against idolatry and polytheism. Much like today, when the moral climate of this nation is at a rapid moral decline and every media outlet is seducing our generations towards other Gods. So God anointed the priesthood for a specific work.

Let's view this in the light of the new testament for a more comprehensive dissection: *But the anointing which ye have received of him abideth in you, and ye need not that any man teach you: but as the same anointing teacheth you of all things, and is truth, and is no lie, and even as it hath taught you, ye shall abide in him. (1 John 2:27)*

First note that in this text John is not denying the importance of good teachers, what he is stating is that neither did the teachers of that day rely on human/carnal wisdom or the opinions of man, to reveal Gods truth but rather their reliance was in the Holy Spirit.

Now let's begin here, *"The anointing which ye have received"* --- if you don't know what the anointing is, you cannot decipher its proper use and purpose and this scripture becomes of no value to you; but the decoding of this text is essential to your spiritual development. We understand the presence of God, is His Glory, but the power of God in mankind is His anointing; and for what this generation is getting ready to see we need both!

The anointing is best described as divine or supernatural ability that helps us to accomplish Gods purposes on the earth. It's doing Gods work with Gods help.

So as we just read, the anointing is used to teach us, and it empowers us to perform in our offices, but because it helps us to function in our roles, many people mistake gifting for anointing.

And here's where the truth comes into play, anyone can operate in ability, gifts and talents, but the anointing, now that is going to cost something. There's a price to pay for the anointing. Your gift, your calling and your anointing are 3 different things. There are no shortcuts to the anointing, this generation is being taught instant gratification, fast food mentality, shortcuts and hacks to everything, but you cannot bypass the process to the anointing.

Meaning, the anointing can't be measured by how good you sang the song, danced the dance, or preached the sermon, the anointing is measured by how Godly you responded when the trials came, (when troubled waters came, did you murmur and complain, did you grumble and bicker? Did you lie, cheat, steal, back-stab, malign and gossip? Or did you display the image and likeness of Christ?)

I'm going to help someone here, the more times you give over to a spirit the more power that spirit has over you, and the more times you give over to the holy spirit, the more predominant is the power of the Holy Spirit working in and through you. Meaning one should live righteously —right thinking, right believing, and right behaving until the Holy Spirit becomes a strong hold!

The anointing is then released through us to allow us to perform our God ordained purpose in the earth realm, but when we don't yield ourselves to the Holy Spirit we can not walk in His power. When we resort to doing things in our own strength, this is what is called works of the flesh, so the anointing and our gifting are not synonymous, we all have spiritual gifts but you must die to you and say yes to God if you want the anointing, that breaks yokes, casts out devils, heals the broken-hearted, and sets the captives free.

Works of the flesh will kill the anointing. Galatians 5:19, *"of which I forewarn you, just as I have forewarned you, that those who practice such things will not inherit the kingdom of God"*.

> ***Prayer and Meditation Scripture:*** But the fruit of the Spirit is love, joy, peace, forbearance, kindness, goodness, faithfulness. Galatians 5:22

Morning Assignment: As you meditate today, be mindful that we are always either operating by the fruit of the spirit or by works of the flesh. One will propagate the anointing, and the other will diminish it. So we must counteract works of the flesh by displaying the fruit of God's spirit, especially when it is trying and difficult. These moment exist to thresh and cull the anointing out of you and release you into a greater dimension and expression of you!

Evening Journal:

*Reflect on Your Morning Assignment and note what happened today as a result of you trying something new. Write about what you **thought** would happen, what **actually** happened, what you **learned**, and what you would do **differently** the next time.*

Notes
Use this area for extra journal space

Notes
Use this area for extra journal space

Shulamite Women Magazine is an online, interactive style magazine covering an array of issues today's believing women are faced with. We publish a generous variety of monthly columns, including topics which span from women's health and fitness, prayer and spirituality, to inner healing, family and relationships, marketplace and much more.

By popular demand, our magazine is now available in a printed format which includes many additional goodies not included on our website, and is printed on beautiful gloss stock quality that is made to last. Each issue will make a beautiful addition to your reading library and make great conversational pieces as receiving table booklets for your home or office.

Subscribe at: www.shulamitewomen.com

www.ingramcontent.com/pod-product-compliance
Lightning Source LLC
Chambersburg PA
CBHW050603300426
44112CB00013B/2048